Louis Harris – Carla Tyler

HOW TO PLAY

SAXOPHONE

IN EASY WAY

A Complete beginner's Guide illustrated Step by Step.

Basics, Features, Easy Instructions, Practice Exercises

to Learn How to Play the Saxophone

Table Of Contents

INTRODUCTION

The saxophone is one of the most youthful musical instruments. It was created by Adolphe Sax, a Belgian, during the 1840s. The saxophone has a sound that is near the human voice, which is the reason it is utilized to communicate feelings. The saxophone frequently praises the French horn, since them two have a comparable range and timbre. A saxophone is as perplexing as a classical instrument yet as eccentric as a non-classical instrument.

The saxophone was initially utilized in the military; however, it is currently a well-known jazz instrument. It is commonly utilized in enormous groups, walking groups, and shows. Saxophones are for the most part identified with jazz since they are utilized generally to play jazz music. Be that as it may, they are likewise utilized for classical music. Saxophone players are called saxophonists.

Saxophones are named woodwind instruments; however, they are commonly made of metal. They are covered with clear or hued veneer. A few saxophones additionally have gold or silver plating. The finish covering assists with forestalling erosion as well as improves the nature of sound and gives a wonderful look to the instrument. The mouthpiece might be made of plastic, elastic, metal, wood or glass. In any case, the material doesn't influence the sound quality. The state of the mouthpiece is found to affect the nature of sound, since those with a curved chamber are felt to deliver milder tones.

The saxophone is like a clarinet, as in both utilize a solitary mouthpiece. In any case, it has a square or adjust cleared inward chamber. The body is cone like fit as a fiddle, like the oboe, however the bend is progressively particular at the chime. Saxophones might be straight or bended, however straight ones are progressively normal.

The fundamental parts in a saxophone are: the mouth-piece including the ligature and the reed;

the principle tube that has tone openings and keys; a progression of bars that interface the keys to the tone gaps; the cushions that safely spread the tone gaps and the chime. The neck tie is additionally significant since saxophones can be extremely overwhelming.

There are a few sorts of saxophones however the four most regular are: Soprano, Alto, Tenor, and Baritone saxophones. The Alto saxophones are littler and perfect for first-time players. They are likewise the most mainstream kind. There are likewise vintage saxophones accessible.

Recycled saxophones can likewise be purchased at a sensible cost. While purchasing a pre-owned saxophone, guarantee that the keys aren't boisterous or spilling. Likewise, check for imprints or scratches. The cushions and the plug ought to be in acceptable working condition. It is smarter to get it checked by an expert before getting it.

The neighborhood music store, mail-request administration, a private gathering or the Internet are potential hotspots for purchasing saxophones.

The fundamental angles to be considered are the quality, administration, cost and the model.

The Internet is a decent spot to discover data about saxophones, yet it is a smart thought to test a couple of them before purchasing.

NOTES ABOUT EQUIPMENT

Some sax players invest an unnecessary measure of energy contemplating equipment...

Tiger Woods would in any case beat you at golf on the off chance that he utilized horrible clubs.

Be that as it may, perhaps not on the off chance that he utilized a polished ash and a volleyball.

So, have ensure your saxophone, mouthpiece, reeds, and so forth are working. Yet, DO NOT invest more energy agonizing over your equipment than really playing and rehearsing.

The saxophone itself has a body and a neck. The mouthpiece goes on the neck and has a reed hung on by a ligature. The mouthpiece, reeds, and ligature matter now and then more than the horn itself.

Saxophone Reeds

The reed makes the sound in your saxophone through its vibration.

Saxophone reeds are made of a unique stick that develops in just a couple of parts of the world. It is costly and wears out in half a month. There are engineered options, however they don't sound as great.

Start with a gentler reed (lower number). What's more, you'll likewise need a gentler reed on the off chance that you have a mouthpiece that is progressively open. Apprentices can begin with number 2 and examination from that point.

Saxophone Mouthpiece

The fundamental thought of mouthpiece position on a sax is that pushing the mouthpiece more remote down on the plug will make your sound higher while hauling it out will make your inflection lower.

To cite Jimmy Haag, "You are fundamentally playing a long cylinder when you play a saxophone. Saxophone is about the speed of the air like any wind instrument. The length of the cylinder decides its sounds. Since EVERYONE has an alternate throat, mouth, teeth, and tongue, it is a genuinely singular excursion to discover what works for you. I meet many individuals who are searching for a standard yet in reality there is just a single way that will work for you."

So, it's not as basic as pushing the mouthpiece on more distant or hauling it out additional.

The temperature and the earth influence inflection as well if it's hot outside the air will move quicker and the sax will be more honed, if its chilly it will in general be level.

Also, a saxophone in order on one note won't really be in order on another note, if not modifications are made by the player. With training, you'll create control and these things will happen subliminally.

Ligature

The ligature holds the reed on the saxophone mouthpiece. It makes a few contrasts. Be that as it may, you most likely don't have to spend silly measures of cash on a precious stone encrusted ligature.

Saxophone Brands

There are four 'major' brands of saxophone:

Selmer, Keilwerth, Yamaha, and Yanagisawa.

They all make proficient horns.

The Selmer Mark VI is the most celebrated kind of saxophone, they quit making them, so the Mark VI's can be extremely expensive nowadays. Be that as it may, numerous experts depend on them. Only one out of every odd Mark VI is still in extraordinary condition, however.

There are some different brands that make better than average horns. Be cautious in the event that they are imported and have delicate metal. What's more, give them a shot before you get them.

Saxophones have highlights, for example, moved tone openings and a high F# key. As a rule, a large number of the headways in instrument making have been embraced by most saxophone organizations.

KINDS OF SAXOPHONE

At the point when you're beginning, play an alto or tenor. Alto's somewhat littler and simpler for a youngster to convey.

Soprano is littler than alto, however its tone is more earnestly to control.

What's more, baritone is bigger than tenor.

Tenor saxophone is the thing that most acclaimed saxophone players favor albeit some favored alto and there are a bunch of saxophone players who for the most part play soprano or baritone.

Soprano Sax

- Mouthpiece
- Ligature
- High octave key
- Neck
- Low octave key
- Neck screw
- Bell

Alto Sax

- Mouthpiece
- High octave key
- Ligature
- Neck
- Neck screw
- Low octave key
- Bell
- Key Guard

Tenor Sax

- Mouthpiece
- Ligature
- Neck
- High octave key
- Neck screw
- Low octave key
- Bell
- Key Guard

Baritone Sax

- Mouthpiece
- Neck
- Ligature
- Low octave key
- High octave key
- Neck screw
- Water Key
- Bell
- Key Guard
- Peg

LEARNING TO PLAY SAXOPHONE

Posture

Hand position

Left hand

Octave key left hand

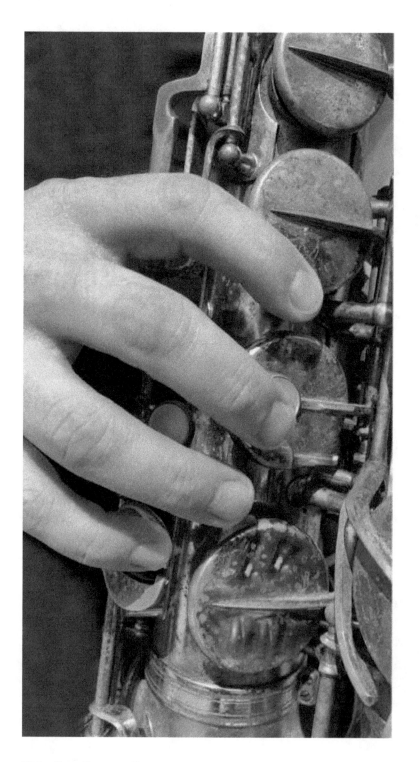

Right hand

Embouchure

There are a wide range of minor departure from instructing great saxophone embouchures. A standard technique includes putting the top teeth on the highest point of the mouthpiece at where the bend of the mouthpiece pulls from the reed. Spread the base teeth with the plump piece of the lower lip to shape a pad. Make pressure around the mouth-piece with the goal that no air escapes from the sides of the mouthpiece. To keep up great sound, the pressure ought to be genuinely reliable right around the mouthpiece, like an elastic band. The embouchure ought to stay reliable for the whole scope of the instrument.

There ought to be no radical development of the jaw to create any note abstain from opening up for low notes or pressing for high notes. The embouchure is commonly reliable, however the tongue position changes in playing distinctive registers. Saxophonists ought to have the option to play all pitches by just delivering a consistent air stream and squeezing fingerings.

Vibrato

Vibrato, included for warmth and expressiveness, is a slight and quick variety in the pitch of a note. It can significantly improve the tone, including a wide variety of hues. It doesn't need to be utilized constantly or at a consistent rate. In the long run the saxophonist will perceive notes and expressions where vibrato is best utilized. While in walking band, vibrato may never be required. In playing huge band gauges, one should imitate a vibrato style of the band that initially played the piece. In show band, con-sider including vibrato as directed by the style of mu-sic. Vibrato can be a priceless instrument for adding life and feeling to saxophone playing.

While rehearsing vibrato, utilize a metronome. To start with, pick a scale and play it in entire notes. Next attempt to modify the tone of each pitch by dropping the jaw multiple times per beat at a metronome stamping of 60 beats for each moment.

The jaw movement for changing the pitch is similar to biting air pocket gum; be that as it may, as one develops rations the strategy, in the long run utilizing only the lip, the plunge of the pitch will turn out to be less recognizable.

Subsequent to building up this activity, work to cause four modifications for every beat, bit by bit moving the metronome increasing to 76. This is around 300 redundancies for every moment. With this office, one can successfully adjust vibrato to change disposition, intensity, and style of a piece.

Play the exercise below at the following oscillations and tempos:

3 pulses at 108 m.m.

4 pulses at 72-80 m.m.

5 pulses at 56-63 m.m.

6 pulses at 48-60 m.m

Vibrato exercises should be played in all keys, as well as the key of G Major is represented above.

The pitch and timbre of certain notes can be very problematic. High A can be exceptionally sharp, center C# very level, and center D and E can be to some degree sharp. These notes should be revised with interchange fingerings or by fixing or slackening the embouchure.

Ask a band chief or private educator about the right utilization of substitute fingerings.

Two standards can manage the tuning of individual pitches:

1)   tighten the embouchure to raise the pitch of a note;

2)   loosen the embouchure to bring down the pitch of a note. Use alert to abstain from upsetting the embouchure so much that it influences the nature of tone.

Sound Concept

Acknowledging how a saxophone should sound ought to be an essential thought when at-enticing to tune and mix with others. The Saxo telephone is flexible and can be played in numerous classifications. Each style has an exceptional jargon because of the sound, explanation, and scales utilized.

So as to appropriately gain proficiency with the musical language of each style one must tune in to the music. Luckily, there are accounts accessible of every kind that can empower an understudy to advance viably. The accounts recorded as prescribed assets later right now can enable the saxophonist to become familiar with the sound concepts for different styles of playing.

Classical saxophone playing is occasionally heard on the radio and is regularly not the sound developed in band; yet, show groups and walking groups use partner require this sort of sound. By and large, classical saxophone playing requires a thick, round, delicious sound. Genuine guides to impersonate would be a horn player, a cellist, or vocalist.

Jazz and jamming are effectively recognized by tuning in to well-known radio. These business styles require a more splendid, edgier sound. Utilize various reeds and mouthpieces (as recently talked about) to help copy these tone ideas.

System

Growing great system on the saxophone will permit one to effectively become familiar with the notes of a bit of music. In the wake of learning the notes and rhythms, concentrate on great tone and musicianship. To have great procedure one must utilize right stance. The back and neck ought to be straight, taking into consideration legitimate relaxing. The neck lash must be pulled up far enough with the goal that the mouthpiece goes to the mouth; don't move the head to the mouthpiece. The tenor and baritone saxophones must be held along the correct leg, even though the alto saxophone can be situated between the legs or to the side. Whichever way is worthy, yet the player must be certain not to lean the instrument against the seat or on the lap; this can change the situation of the mouth-piece in the mouth. The saxophone is essentially sup-ported by the neck lash and the left and right thumbs. The correct thumb is put in the thumb protect so the hand can delicately bend with the fingertips on the pearls. The correct pinky finger is set where the Eb and C keys meet with the goal that they can be utilized rapidly. The left thumb goes about as a balance to hold your instrument set up. The thumb ought to be set with the goal that it can without much of a stretch come to the octave key. The remainder of the left hand is bent around the palm keys with the goal that the fingertips contact the pearls. The left pinky is set on the G# key so it very well may be utilized rapidly. It is imperative to keep the fingers that are not being utilized as near the keys as could reasonably be expected. When playing centre C#, where no keys are de-squeezed, all fingertips ought to be contacting the pearls. Keeping fingers near the keys disposes of squandered movement and permits increasingly quick development between notes. Another model happens when playing a low G. The three remaining fingers ought to be down and the left pinky should contact the G# key. The fingers of the correct hand ought to lay on the pearls.

While in secondary school the saxophonist ought to endeavor to become familiar with all major, consonant minor, and chromatic scales over the full length of the instrument (allude to Example 1 and Scale Supplement). Scales are a piece of the language of music. On the off chance that one knows the scales, they can be effectively recognized as music is perused. Practically all music depends on some scale. On the off chance that one perceives scales, playing pieces will be simpler and making music will be increasingly fun.

To be viable, specialized learning must be moderate and efficient. Gradually instruct the fingers what they must do. Building up a decent practice schedule, setting short and long haul objectives, and utilizing productive basic reasoning will assist one with turning into an increasingly cultivated saxophonist.

Tonguing

Tonguing alludes to the manner in which the saxophonist explains specific notes and rhythms. The tongue can deliver light staccato, substantial marcato, long legato, accentuated highlights, and a lot more sounds. The more assortment of music played, the more sorts of verbalization experienced. When all is said in done, the saxophonist makes the syllable to be delivered with the tongue before sounding the note. Utilize the syllables "doo," "dah," or "dee" for a lighter tongue, "tah" or "tee" for a heavier tongue. The tip is angled forward and, as the syllable is delivered, the piece of the tongue somewhat over its tip contacts the tip of the reed quickly obstructs the air and makes the note be rearticulated when discharged. The air stream stays relentless, ceaselessly. Issues with tonguing emerge if a lot of the outside of the tongue contacts the reed; a slapping, thuddy sound outcomes. Tonguing ought to be drilled with scales and intentions. Regularly, the hardest piece of consummating a specialized tonguing entry is planning the tongue with the fingers.

The speed of the tongue can be created by doing activities to fortify the tongue.

While doing any activity for speed, utilize a metronome to abstain from hurrying or hauling. Ensure the explanation is clear and address without fail. When setting a beat, decide at what speed an entry can be neatly tongued; at that point gradually speed up the metronome. Work on tonguing in each register of the instrument, as each range will change accordingly time.

Accents are played simply like ordinary notes aside from that an additional push of air is added to accentuate the note. Use alert to abstain from detonating assaults.

The best way to deal with tonguing is the accomplishment of good legato tonguing, which will prompt a decent staccato tongue.

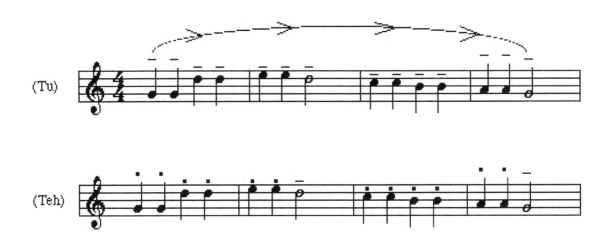

Here we utilize the stomach muscles to kick the air "ha" with the tongue "teh" so it is "teh" not "tut". The musical impact we need here is light and decreased staccato.

The air must beginning quick and unexpectedly, however stop gradually or decreased like a pizzicato or pluck of a string.

Exercises in Legato Tonguing

Light touch tongue all air. It should sound almost like you are sustaining a note.

Legato Tonguing

"dit" or "tet"

Exercises in Staccato Tonguing

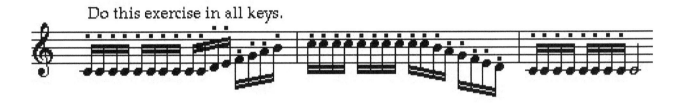

5 Half Tones

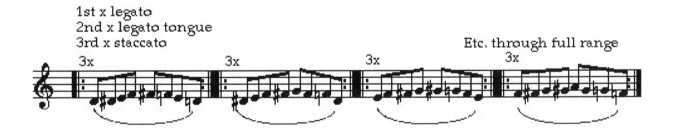

*When playing chromatic sections utilize the trill F# key just as the side C. In the event that the chromatic scale is inside the setting of a moderate melodic line, utilize normal F# and C.

Additional Tonguing Exercises

Play the exercises below in all keys. Start on the tonic or root and descend one octave.

Repeat the same exercise ascending one octave as detailed below.

Intonation

All saxophones have pitch irregularities that must be recognized and made up for so as to accomplish great intonation. No two saxophones are the equivalent, albeit some are superior to other people.

Be that as it may, different registers of all instruments do have comparable inclinations. Regularly, low Bb through low D# are sharp, low E through center C# are level, and center D through high F is sharp. A considerable lot of the components talked about in before areas, (for example, mouthpiece, reed, state of the instrument, and air support) can enormously influence the intonation.

Interpretation

A saxophonist as a musician must understand that music is something other than notes. Focus on tone, intonation, and the markings on the music.

All imprinting's are composed which is as it should be. Elements, intonations, crescendos, and so on., should be perceptible to the crowd. Music is contained differentiation, so accentuate vary fences.

In the wake of deciphering the markings, utilize individual taste, the conductor, or a private educator to refine how the music ought to be performed. Misrepresent these markings and refine them in practice, striving for a charming musical presentation.

INSTRUMENT MAINTENANCE

Saxophones resemble without ordinary maintenance, they won't react well to your activities. An ineffectively kept up instrument can make its player sound terrible, have a ton of fun, and become disappointed rapidly. Regular issues incorporate defective cushions, bowed keys and bars, missing felts and plugs, broken springs, unregulated keys, and flawed arrangement.

Saxophonists can do numerous things to keep their instruments in great playing condition. In the first place, clear the dampness out of the saxophone neck and body subsequent to playing. This will help expel the buildup from the drag and cushions, permitting them to dry quicker. Inability to do this normally can make cushions destroy rapidly. The instrument may likewise build up a disagreeable blue microorganisms may even develop on the cushions and bore! Second, utilize two hands when holding or moving the instrument, particularly while getting it out or taking care of it. Be particularly mindful so as not to twist the bars. Third, investigate the instrument consistently. Search for free cushions, broke plugs, and irregular snaps; have them checked before they become serious issues. At last, have the instrument assessed intermittently by a certified proficient repairman. Doing this safeguard maintenance in any event once a year will fix numerous minor issues and take out the requirement for exorbitant significant fixes later.

Recall that an appropriately kept up instrument will work better and be progressively enjoyable to play.

Breath Support

The lungs must be prepared to deliver the consistent, engaged, continued air stream expected to make vibrations in the reed and mouthpiece. Great stance with a straight back and neck will significantly help the breathing procedure. Try not to raise and lower the shoulders when breathing. Lifting the shoulders makes pressure that will influence the sound and the fingers. Players should attempt to utilize their whole lung limit, permitting the lower some portion of the lungs to push the stomach forward, at that point filling the upper pit. The air is then discharged relentlessly, constrained by a muscle called the stomach. The airstream ought to consistently be relentless, never rough.

A player can consider filling the instrument or the entire room, never halting the air aside from toward the finish of an expression or during rest. Utilizing too little air can bring about playing sharp while utilizing an excessive amount of air can make a note go level. A decent method to work on creating a consistent air stream is to play scales at different paces utilizing the full scope of the instrument. Focus on creating an even air stream and predictable sound as far as possible all over.

Mouthpieces and reeds

There is a wide range of sorts of reeds and mouthpieces created for the differing styles of music a saxophonist must play. For the most part, a medium-sized mouthpiece will meet most walking and show band needs. A medium confronting will star duce a round, centered sound regularly required for these gatherings. The mouthpiece will help in mixing with the dynamic, tone shading, and style of different musicians. A Selmer C★ is a standout amongst other medium-sized mouthpieces. Whenever cost or accessibility is a problem, it ought to be noticed that most mouthpieces that accompany another instrument have a medium confronting and will be satisfactory. When acting in jazz gatherings, a mouthpiece with a bigger tip opening might be expected to extend the sound and match the flexible styles and more brilliant timbre of the other musicians. Great mouthpieces and facings for this style incorporate Meyer 5, 6, or 7 or Otto Link 5, 6, or 7. Mouthpieces are generally made of hard elastic or metal. These materials produce various timbres and have favorable circumstances and drawbacks. Settle on an informed decision when picking a mouth-piece. Utilize the information on a band chief, private instructor, nearby expert musician, or music seller to discover a match that will suit the playing needs. In any case, recollect that the cost of a mouthpiece has little to do with its reasonableness.

It is essential to coordinate the quality of the reed to the mouthpiece. The airstream blows against the mouthpiece/reed arrangement, making the vibrations that become the sound. Reeds that are too delicate will create low notes too effectively, cause high notes to be off-key, and sound halted and soft. Delicate reeds may support utilizing a frail air stream or poor embouchure to create the sound.

The reed will vibrate too effectively and unusually against the mouthpiece, so the focal point of the sound and pitch will consistently vary. Hard reeds, which require extreme measures of air to make them vibrate, may hamper low note playing, energize a gnawing embouchure, and advance over the top air use. Select a reed quality that will deliver a sound that has a reliable tone all through the full scope of the instrument. Octaves and interims ought to be changed just with fingerings, not with foolish throat and embouchure development (See Example 2 on page 3).

By and large, a medium quality reed fits a medium mouthpiece confronting. For instance, 3 or 31/2 Vandoren reeds would fit a Selmer C★ mouthpiece. A lower quality reed fits an enormous, open mouthpiece (i.e., 2 or 21/2 reeds may better match a Meyer 7 mouthpiece). Counsel a band executive, private educator, or expert for help in coordinating the reed to the mouthpiece. Remember that reed qualities fluctuate between producers—a #3 Vandoren reed, a #3 Rico reed, and a #3 Rico Royal reed are altogether different.

The ligature is a significant piece of the mouth-piece/reed arrangement, which can likewise substantially affect tone. Ensure the ligature is inacceptable condition, taking into consideration a cosy attack of the reed against the mouthpiece. Ligatures that are twisted, broken, or missing screws may work to a constrained degree, however, don't let the reed vibrate accurately against the mouthpiece.

Mouthpieces and reeds Care

Make certain to routinely clear out the mouthpiece with a delicate fabric, not a brush. This cleaning will keep murmurs and outside articles from decreasing or changing vibrations in the chamber. Exercise care to abstain from chipping the tip or scratching the drag and rails of the mouthpiece.

Saxophonists ought to keep up at least four playable reeds consistently. Reeds that are waterlogged, chipped, broke, or shrouded in lipstick ought not be played.

When taking care of the saxophone, don't leave a reed on the mouthpiece. It can without much of a stretch chip, become stained, and build up an unsavory smell. Reeds ought to be put away in a reed protect or—at smaller than normal mum the plastic covers that accompany a few reeds. This will protect them until the following use and they will dry uniformly without distorting. A reed watchman can be produced using a bit of glass, with adjusted sides for wellbeing, with elastic groups to hold the reeds set up. Reeds ought to be turned frequently, permitting them to dry out appropriately and last more; this will cost less over the long haul because less reeds will be required.

Saxophone FAQs

1. How old do I need to be to begin playing saxophone?

By and large if you are 10 years old or more established you will be sufficiently large to begin playing the Alto saxophone. For more youthful understudies the Alto is unquestionably the best decision. Even though the Soprano sax is littler it is a lot harder to play and requires more control in your mouth. If you are enormous for your age, at that point maybe you could begin somewhat more youthful however you should have the option to hold the heaviness of the saxophone and have enough puff to make a sound! A few instructors prescribe beginning on recorder first to get the general thought of the fingering as the notes on the comment or soprano recorder are equivalent to low enroll of the saxophone.

2. Which size saxophone would it be a good idea for me to begin with?

The Alto is commonly the best size saxophone to begin on for the novice player. Even though the Soprano is a littler instrument it requires significantly more control and is precarious to gain snappy ground on for the fledgling saxophone player. The tenor is a lot heavier than the Alto so is progressively appropriate to a grown-up or tall adolescent to begin on. The extraordinary thing about saxophones however is that the fingering (or way you play the notes) is the equivalent on every one of them so once you get the hang of an Alto for instance, it's generally simple to then change to a tenor, soprano or baritone.

3. I have little hands - would i be able to even now play the saxophone?

I have met phenomenal players who have little hands - it extremely just boils down to becoming accustomed to the instrument. Notwithstanding, you might be better beginning the Alto first as the keys are nearer together than on a Tenor.

4. What amount do I need to spend to get an average starter sax?

There is a wide scope of starter saxophones available. You can pay as meager as £170 for another understudy instrument up to more than £800 for a portion of the more settled brands. In spite of the fact that you can expect some distinction in quality over this value go, a large number of the less expensive instruments will offer awesome assistance for a learner saxophone player at an increasingly open cost. Nowadays the distinction in quality right now is negligible as most brands fabricate their instruments right now in China or Taiwan. The other interesting point is that as your playing creates you will most likely need to advance on to a further developed instrument or maybe change from Alto to Tenor so it might merit considering a starter sax as an initial step on your musical excursion.

5. Will my sax need standard support?

Each saxophone will require an "adjust" now and again. Saxophones have functional parts like cushions and plugs that with normal use will require alteration and conceivable substitution. On the off chance that your saxophone starts to be difficult to play, or a few notes won't sound appropriately then you will presumably need to get it adjusted. Fortunately getting your saxophone fixed is reasonable (presumably under £40) and on the off chance that you take great consideration of your instrument you may just need to do this once consistently.

6. My sax isn't working accurately - how might I get it fixed?

There are numerous nearby instrument repairers in the UK. Your nearby music shop can by and large prescribe a decent repairer. If you have taken great consideration of your instrument, at that point most issues that happen are effectively fixed and not over the top expensive.

7. What size reeds do I need?

Reeds arrive in a scope of sizes beginning at 1½ and going up in ½ steps to around 4. The numbers demonstrate how thick the reeds are cut thus that they are so difficult to play. As an amateur saxophone player, you should begin a size 1½ reed and climb to a size 2 when you discover blowing extremely simple. If you are rehearsing hard you will before long find that your sound is very slender with a size 1½ reed - this is a decent sign that the time has come to move onto size 2. As you create as a player you will locate the size that suits you best and is a decent counterpart for your mouthpiece. Something else to consider is that you will likely break a ton of reeds when you are simply beginning - reeds are exceptionally delicate and do wear out so anticipate that a decent reed should possibly last around 1-2 weeks or less if you are playing routinely.

8. My sax squeaks a great deal when I blow - am I accomplishing something incorrectly?

There could be various purposes behind this. First beginning by checking your reed is on effectively, is wet and doesn't have any significant chips or splits in it. At that point, be certain that when you play you have your base lip over your teeth (your base teeth ought to never contact the reed). Likewise, take a stab at trying different things with utilizing less mouthpiece when you play. Some of the time an excess of mouthpiece can cause squeaks. Lastly, if all these don't fix the issue, at that point quite possibly your sax needs the consideration of a repairer!

9. Where would I be able to discover exercises to kick me off?

There are some amazing instructional DVDs that can give you pointers to begin yet maybe the best thing is to consolidate this with certain exercises from an accomplished instructor to get the key aptitudes right. When learning an instrument, it is extremely essential to get the fundamental aptitudes directly toward the begin to give you the most obvious opportunity with regards to having achievement later.

10. What would i be able to do to update my Sax?

Probably the best moves up to consider with a novice saxophone is changing the mouthpiece. The mouthpiece is the primary spot the sound is made on the saxophone and it's quality can have a huge effect not exclusively to the sound you make however how simple your sax is to play. Most saxes (even some middle of the road or propelled saxes) come sent with an essential mouthpiece. While this is alright to kick you off, you will most likely discover redesigning it will have a major effect to the nature of your sound and how your sax feels when playing. There are heaps of mouthpieces available. For an apprentice saxophone player, you should seriously mull over either a Yamaha 4C (about £30) or a Selmer C* (about £80). Both are made of plastic/bakelite and are broadly considered as amazing mouthpieces. As you're playing creates you should try different things with different brands and sizes to make your own sound. When all is said in done mouthpieces made or plastic or bakelite (dark ones) are useful for an increasingly controlled, classical smooth sound, though metal mouthpieces (either gold or silver/chrome) will give you a lot more splendid and stronger sound. Do some Google to find what mouthpiece your preferred player employments!

11. How might I tell a decent sax from a terrible sax?

This is a generally excellent inquiry. It very well may be difficult to tell what to search for if you are new to saxophone. Awful instances of lower valued instruments for the most part experience the ill effects of poor form quality (as you may anticipate). Have a nearby take a gander at the saxophone for flaws in the polish/plating, additionally search for bowed or screwy keys and clearly any imprints or indications of misuse. Another sax ought to consistently be checked and "set up" before conveyance to you. On the off chance that you are having trouble playing another sax don't spare a moment to take it back and get an accomplished repairer to check it. All around most issues on saxophones can be effectively helped by a decent repairer. To make things increasingly entangled, cost isn't constantly a decent pointer of value either. Nowadays there are some great lower valued saxes for the tenderfoot saxophone player and some overestimated instruments with issues so consistently search for certain audits from companions or on the web if you are uncertain.

12. To what extent will a saxophone last my kid?

A fair instrument that is all around thought about and normally kept up should keep going for quite a long while. Numerous understudies progress directly through their evaluations on a better than average understudy instrument some advancing to college level. In the end as you're playing creates and spending plan permits you may decide to move up to an expert instrument and when you arrive at this point you will be better ready to choose what is the correct instrument for you.

Practice Exercises:

House of the Rising Sun

We Wish You a Merry Christmas

trad.

Joy to the World

O Holy Night

Trad.

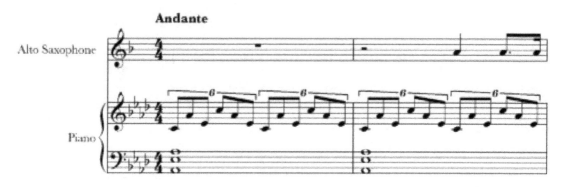

Books by the same author:

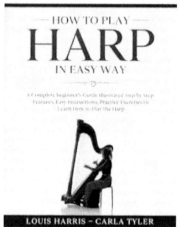

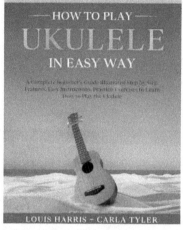

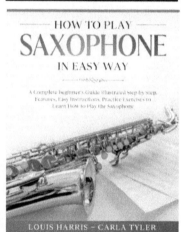
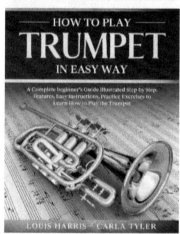

Search: "Louis Harris"
on Amazon

Kind reader,

Thank you very much. I hope you enjoyed the book. Can I ask you a big favor?

I would be grateful if you would please take a few minutes to leave me a gold star on Amazon.

Thank you again for your support.

Louis Harris

Printed in the USA
CPSIA information can be obtained
at www.ICGtesting.com
LVHW071603081223
765952LV00003B/63